Prompts & Practices

JUDY REEVES

New World Library
Novato, California

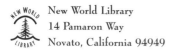

New World Library
14 Pamaron Way
Novato, California 94949

Package © 2003 Judy Reeves
Text excerpted from *A Writer's Book of Days* © 1999 Judy Reeves

Edited by Vanessa Brown
Package design by Mary Ann Casler
Text design and typography by Tona Pearce Myers

First Printing October 2003
Package ISBN 1-57731-435-2
Printed in Thailand
Distributed by Publishers Group West

10 9 8 7 6 5 4 3 2

Throw yourself into the hurly-burly of life.
It doesn't matter how many mistakes you make,
what unhappiness you have to undergo.
It is all your material.
Don't wait for experience to come to you;
go out after experience.
Experience is your material.

— W. Somerset Maugham

Introduction

The idea of writing practice is a new concept to many who want to write. Sure, everybody knows pianists have to train. So do dancers, actors, singers, and athletes. Even artists have sketchbooks, which serve as their practice pages. But there seems to be some vague notion that somewhere deep inside the desire to be a writer is the inherent knowledge of how to go about it. Many a bloody-fingered would-be writer, hip-deep in wadded-up paper and frustration can attest, that this just ain't so.

Natural talent and all the breaks in the world notwithstanding, to become good at anything you've got to do the drills. Lots of drills. To quote Mick Jagger, "You have to sing every day so you can build up to being, you know, *amazingly brilliant.*"

A stranger to New York City, looking for directions, asks a man on the street, "How do I get to Carnegie Hall?"

"Practice, man," comes the response. It's an old joke, but the truth is there. In order to get good at anything, you've got to practice. So when somebody asks me, How do I write a novel? Or a short story? An essay, poem, or book? I give them the same answer as that man on the street: practice, practice, practice.

Writing Practice

Writing practice is showing up at the page. It's running the scales, executing the movements. It's writing for the experience of it, forming the words, capturing the images, filling the pages.

Like an artist's sketchbook, a writer's notebook is filled with perspectives, character sketches, shadings, and tones. A writing workout is trying out phrases and auditioning words, letting the imagination have free rein while the editor in your head takes a coffee break. One of the best things about writing practice is that it is practice. It's not supposed to be perfect. You're free to make mistakes, fool around, take risks.

When you show up at the page and put in the time day after day, you learn to trust your pen and the voice that emerges as your own. You name yourself Writer.

By taking the time for writing practice, you are honoring yourself as writer. When you write on a daily basis, your self-confidence increases. You learn what you want to write about and what matters to you as a writer. You explore your creative nooks and crannies, and make forays into some scary places that make your hand tremble and your heart beat faster. This is good. This is when you know you are writing your truth, and that's the best writing anybody ever does. In writing practice, you poke around in your psyche; you grieve and heal and discover things about yourself you never knew. And this is the truth: your writing really does get better.

Make a Commitment by Making the Time

Talking about writing isn't the same as writing. Anyone who has promised herself she'd go to the gym today "no matter what" then finds herself still in her office clothes at 10 P.M. knows this. "I'll do it tomorrow," the would-be exerciser says day after day, just like the would-be writer.

The way to make a commitment to writing practice is to make an appointment with your writer-self and keep it — same as you would an appointment with your dentist or your best friend. Write in your daily calendar the time each day you plan to write. Ten minutes or two hours. Write it down. Then do it.

You may have to change your appointment. Certainly there will be days when, no matter what, you simply have to cancel. When this happens, do it consciously and with intention. Just as you would call your dentist or best friend to reschedule rather than standing them up, tell yourself why you have to postpone or change the appointment, and set a time for another meeting. Your writer-self deserves this consideration.

Getting into a regular practice groove may take a few test runs. You may schedule mornings when nights are really better. If you commit to two hours every day, but find yourself stressed-out and hating the idea of writing practice and going to the page with a Godzilla-sized grudge, or, worse yet, not going at all, reconsider how much time you can really commit. Be flexible. Create a schedule that works for you, so that when practice time comes, you accept it as an ongoing, necessary part of your life as a writer and look forward to it as a gift to yourself.

Writing Prompts

Many writing practitioners, when they sit down to write, freeze. "I don't know what to write about," they say, while holding the pen in a death grip somewhere down near the nib. Truth is, each of us has so much we want to write about, a deluge of ideas, memories, and images, that we can become paralyzed by infinite choice. The brain simply can't make up its mind so it launches into what it does best: measuring, judging, calculating. Thinking. The worst possible thing for writing practice.

This is why I've provided suggested writing topics for each day of the year. The topics follow, two weeks' worth on each page. To use this book, simply locate the date, write the topic for that day at the top of a blank page in this book, or in a separate notebook, grab the first image that comes to you, and write it. No matter what the topic, what you want to write about will emerge on the page. Story seedlings, poetic uprisings, character visitations — things that are deep inside are brought to the surface by the focus and energy and freewheeling fearlessness of writing practice.

When you write from the topics, feel free to change the tense — past to present or vice versa — or the point of view. If the topic uses "you," this doesn't mean you have to write about yourself. Change the pronoun to "he" or "she," or use a character's name (or a real person, if you want). Use the prompts to write from a character's point of view; create a fragment or work on a scene for a longer piece. Write fiction, memoir, essay. Mix the genres; find your writer's groove, then ride it.

The writing topics are expressed in several ways — as sentence stems, quotes, directives, or simply phrases or words.

For example, the topic for January 16 is a simple, straightforward directive: *Write about a bed*. If the first image that comes to you is the bed you slept in when you were ten in your messy, toy-strewn childhood bedroom with the flowered wallpaper, write about that bed. Begin anywhere — going to sleep, waking up, changing the sheets, hiding beneath the covers. If you're writing a fictional piece, write about a bed from a character's point of view, whatever bed the character "sees." Write an essay on beds, an homage to beds, an ode to your lover's bed, or a list poem of beds you have slept in (or not). The invitation is as broad as a king-size mattress and as unlimited as anything you might dream thereon.

The topic for March 28 is a sentence stem: *"The last time I saw_____."* Because the prompt is set in quotes, it invites you to use the sentence as dialogue, but you don't have to write dialogue. Simply begin with the sentence stem, fill in the blank with the first image that comes to you, and be off on a ten-minute romp through a city, with a person, on a riverboat, at the theater, or in the company of your favorite nephew or the ice cream vendor.

On November 13, a line from a poem by Wisława Szymborska is used: *"The window had other views."* Throughout the book, great writers are quoted, sometimes, as in this case, with a line for a writing prompt. When writing from this topic, it's not necessary to actually use the line in your writing. Use instead the images it suggests, looking out the windows of your memory or imagination, or the window you sit before as you write. Of course, you can use the line anywhere in the piece, even as a line of dialogue or the lead-in to start your writing.

You're in the backseat of a taxi is the prompt for March 19. This topic can be written from the second person (you), or it can be about yourself (a memory of being in the backseat of a taxi), or it can be about a fictional character. Again, take the image that comes from the prompt, without taking the prompt too literally.

One more example: the topic for January 13 is *After midnight.* The lack of any directive (*write about, describe, remember*) is intentional. You're free to use the actual words as the beginning of a sentence, or to find inspiration in the idea of "after midnight," as a time, space, feeling, or image. Or write an after midnight memory.

Prompts aren't themes for compositions or essays. They're not topics you must stay with, as in "stick to the topic." The idea is not to think about what the prompts mean or how to interpret them. Just start writing. The freedom to let your writing go down any open road is one of the delights of writing to suggested topics. You don't even have to use the prompt itself!

Different writers respond to different invitations. Some writers resonate with concrete images, others like abstract. And often, the less said about a prompt, the more wide-open the invitation for the intuitive to work. A sentence stem one day, an evocative quote the next, sometimes just an image — this variety stimulates writerly interest and keeps the prompts fresh. Don't worry about "doing it right." The good news is there's no way to do it wrong. Simply read the prompt, trust the image, and begin writing.

You can use the topics again and again; different images will emerge, memories will rise, fresh ideas will form, and you'll keep writing. After some time, you'll be able to reread your notebooks and notice themes and recurring images. This is another gift of writing practice: you'll discover what matters to you as a writer, what you are passionate about.

An important note about the topics: don't reject the topic out of hand or consider what you're going to write about before you begin. Find the topic, note it at the top of your page, and begin writing. If you stop to think, you'll run the risk of talking yourself out of what might be a rich vein for writing-practice mining.

This kit provides prompts for every day of the year, ample pages for writing sessions, and instructive cards to guide your practice. Pick from the deck at random, select a favorite exercise, or find an especially needed focus. Most importantly, embrace the process and enjoy yourself.

The Effects of Writing Practice

I've been leading writing-practice groups for nearly a decade, two and three times a week, as well as writing marathons that run long hours, and I always write along with the others. I have also participated in countless practice sessions alone, with various writing partners, and with a mélange of writing groups.

On any given day, a writer can write the best she's ever written, or she can compose a piece that's clunky and misshapen and downright embarrassing in its black-and-white awfulness. Practice isn't about being a good writer or a bad writer, it's about being present with the writing, surrendering to the process, and trusting the pen.

At any given practice session, we are all beginners.

Through writing practice, I have been invited to participate in a community where I am free to be all that I am as writer — insecure, self-conscious, awkward, passionate, raw, reckless, wild, and even outside myself. I have found my own kind.

By showing up at the page and doing the writing, I and other writers have filled hundreds of notebooks. We have started and completed short stories, plays, novels, essays, memoirs, gifts of writing for others, and, wondrously, we have even experienced the appearance of poems. We've claimed ourselves as writers.

If you will practice every day, and be gentle with yourself, you may be amazed. Your writing will be fresher, livelier, more spontaneous. You will take more risks, write more passionately, and reach into places you didn't know existed. Ideas and images and language with brilliant plumage will parade on the page before your eyes. Then one day, after a particularly surprising session, you will read what you have written, shake your head in astonishment, and say, "Where did that come from?" And you will know, it came from you.

Guidelines for Writing Practice

1. Keep writing. Don't stop to edit, to rephrase, to think. Don't go back and read what you've written until you've finished.
2. Trust your pen. Go with the first image that appears.
3. Don't judge your writing. Don't compare, analyze, criticize.
4. Let your writing find its own form. Allow it to organically take shape into a story, an essay, a poem, dialogue, an incomplete meander.
5. Don't worry about the rules. Don't worry about grammar, syntax, punctuation, or sentence structure.
6. Let go of expectations. Let your writing surprise you.
7. Kiss your frogs. Remember, this is just practice. Not every session will be magic. The point is to just suit up and show up at the page, no matter what.
8. Tell the truth. Be willing to go to the scary places that make your hand tremble and your handwriting get a little out of control. Be willing to tell your secrets.
9. Write specific details. Your writing doesn't have to be factual, but the specificity of the details brings it alive. The truth isn't in the facts; it's in the detail.
10. Write what matters. If you don't care about what you're writing, neither will your readers. Be a passionate writer.
11. Read your writing aloud after you've completed your practice session. You'll find out what you've written, what you care about, when you're writing the truth, and when the writing is "working."
12. Date your page and write the topic at the top. This will keep you grounded in the present and help you reference pieces you might want to use in something else.

A Year of *Writing* Prompts

What is important?
Living as active a life as possible,
meeting all ranks of people, plenty of travel,
trying your hand at various kinds of work,
keeping your eyes, ears, and mind open,
remembering what you observe,
reading plenty of good books,
and writing every day—simply writing.

— Edward Abbey

Don't just put in your time.
That is not enough.
You have to make a great effort.
Be willing to put your whole life on the line
when you sit down for writing-practice.

— Natalie Goldberg

anuary

January	1	Write about Sunday afternoon.
January	2	Write about a time someone said no.
January	3	You're standing in a doorway.
January	4	"A year after your death..." (after Czeslaw Milosz)
January	5	Write about a day moon.
January	6	Write about bathing.
January	7	Once, when no one was looking...
January	8	It's what I do in the middle of the night.
January	9	Write about a ceremony.
January	10	Write about a wound.
January	11	You are in a motel room.
January	12	Write about acceptable losses.
January	13	After midnight.
January	14	Write about the horizon.
January	15	It's Saturday afternoon. You're not at home.

January 16	Write about a bed.
January 17	Write about a time you found out about something you weren't supposed to know.
January 18	"It was noon and nothing is concluded." (after Donald Rawley)
January 19	Remember a sound.
January 20	Look out your window; write what you see.
January 21	Write about something you bought mail order.
January 22	In the meantime...
January 23	Write a love letter. To anyone.
January 24	Write about leaving.
January 25	Shadows.
January 26	Describe the contents of someone's closet.
January 27	Write about a used car.
January 28	Write about "the sky you were born under." (after Joy Harjo)
January 29	The end of the day.
January 30	Write about a forbidden activity.
January 31	"The first time I wore _____."

February

February	1	Write about a kiss.
February	2	Find your way in a city.
February	3	These are the things women know about love.
February	4	Write about a black and white photograph.
February	5	"When I awoke the next morning..."
February	6	Write about a stranger.
February	7	"Everybody loves the sound of a train in the distance. Everybody thinks it's true." (after Paul Simon)
February	8	Write about a river.
February	9	Write about a wild-eyed dream.
February	10	You hear church bells in the distance.
February	11	This is how my heart was broken.
February	12	Write your morning.
February	13	You're moving into a new house; write about the people or person who lived there before you.

February 14   Write about the night sky.

February 15   Write about a brief encounter.

February 16   Someone gave you flowers.

February 17   Open the box.

February 18   Blue — the color or the emotion.

February 19   Write about a quilt or a blanket.

February 20   Close your eyes. Write about what you see.

February 21   Someone's playing the radio.

February 22   Write about a tattoo.

February 23   These are the pleasures I have known.

February 24   Once, in the midst of all the recklessness . . .

February 25   "By the sea, beneath the yellow and
               sagging moon."
               (after Walt Whitman)

February 26   The last time.

February 27   Write about fireworks.

February 28   What if . . .

February 29   Write about a balcony.

March

March	1	Write about hair.
March	2	This much is known…
March	3	You see a shooting star.
March	4	"At 5 in the afternoon." (after Federico García Lorca)
March	5	What are you waiting for?
March	6	Write about someone who left.
March	7	Write about a time you won big.
March	8	Night.
March	9	Write about a secret revealed.
March	10	Give me a moon story.
March	11	"You have stayed too long."
March	12	Write about stealing something.
March	13	Write about a longing.
March	14	Write about a justifiable sin.
March	15	"If I had my way…"

March 16	Write about small injuries.
March 17	On the eve of the funeral.
March 18	Write about promises that were broken.
March 19	You're in the backseat of a taxi.
March 20	This is a map to where I live.
March 21	Write about a fortune-teller.
March 22	Write about taking the long way around.
March 23	"I remember how it was to drive in gravel." (after Theodore Roethke)
March 24	Write about getting caught in the act.
March 25	Write what you didn't do.
March 26	There were signs and signals.
March 27	Write about memories underfoot.
March 28	"The last time I saw _____ ,"
March 29	Write about something astonishing.
March 30	"So, these were my friends..." (after John Balaban)
March 31	Every morning...

April

April 16	Write about falling from grace.
April 17	Write about what's under your house.
April 18	Just beyond the edge of the woods.
April 19	Write about a time you did something you didn't want to do.
April 20	Write about meeting someone for the first time.
April 21	Something seemed different.
April 22	This is not about...
April 23	One thing can't be denied...
April 24	Write about a year ago.
April 25	You hear music in the background.
April 26	Once, with another woman...
April 27	"I can never say quite as much as I know." (after Robert Olen Butler)
April 28	Write about a time you wanted to leave, but couldn't.
April 29	Write about secrets revealed.
April 30	Write about an injury.

May

May 15	Write about a reflection.
May 16	Ten years ago…
May 17	You're in a hotel lobby.
May 18	Write about a place you know, but not well.
May 19	One day…
May 20	Write about ebb tide.
May 21	It's too soon to tell.
May 22	Write about predictability.
May 23	Road maps.
May 24	Write about something you see every day.
May 25	You're listening to the radio.
May 26	"And it was at that age…" (after Pablo Neruda)
May 27	It's snowing.
May 28	Write about a time someone said yes.
May 29	Before I was born.
May 30	If I could do it over again.
May 31	You hear a siren.

June

June	1	Write about something to hold onto.
June	2	Write about a silence.
June	3	Once, when I was...
June	4	What are you looking for?
June	5	Write about small regrets.
June	6	You are standing on one side of a closed door.
June	7	Write about something that came in a box.
June	8	This is the voice of my body.
June	9	Rising early to begin the journey.
June	10	Write about a compromise.
June	11	Write about mistaken identity.
June	12	"Afterward, I thought about..."
June	13	These were the doubts I had.

June 14	Write about a dinner party.
June 15	When the dust settles.
June 16	Write about an island.
June 17	It's who you met at a party.
June 18	Out of the corner of my eye.
June 19	In the heat of the afternoon.
June 20	Someone's playing the piano.
June 21	Write about a pair of shoes.
June 22	Write about a letter.
June 23	Write about an hour of the day.
June 24	This is what you can see by starlight.
June 25	It was Sunday, the time it happened.
June 26	Write about the making of beds.
June 27	This is where I went wrong.
June 28	Write about small change.
June 29	Write about high tide.
June 30	"Long afterward, I came upon it again..." (after Colette)

July

July 1   The possibilities are endless.

July 2   These were the frequently asked questions.

July 3   Write about the inevitable.

July 4   Write about a voice.

July 5   Write about a time you cried.

July 6   So it has come to this.

July 7   It was his idea of a good time.

July 8   Write about a gate.

July 9   Write what you wanted to do.

July 10   Write about a postcard.

July 11   It was as if . . .

July 12   "Throw away the lights, the definitions
and say of what you see in the dark."
(after Wallace Stevens)

July 13   Write about a theft.

July 14   Write about an epiphany.

July 15	It was that kind of day.
July 16	Half an hour before sunrise.
July 17	In a state of disarray.
July 18	Write about a recurring dream.
July 19	Write about a time you got what you wanted.
July 20	Write about passing time.
July 21	Write about packing a suitcase.
July 22	The first time I saw _____.
July 23	Write about being late.
July 24	Write about a conversation.
July 25	Write about asking for mercy.
July 26	A free-for-all.
July 27	You're in a movie theater.
July 28	Every night...
July 29	Write about a scent.
July 30	Write about an eclipse.
July 31	Somebody makes a promise.

ugust

August   1   Write about a tool.

August   2   Write about a time you were misunderstood.

August   3   Write about a bedroom.

August   4   If only...

August   5   Write about a summer night.

August   6   "I was listening to something I heard before."

August   7   Someone is calling your name.

August   8   Write about something that was stolen.

August   9   On the other side.

August   10   I've never seen his face.

August   11   This is what the neighbors saw.

August   12   Something's burning.

August   13   And when autumn finally arrived.

August   14   Write about the careless days.

August   15   Aftershocks of the full moon.

August 16	"Sleeping Where I Fall." (after Peter Coyote)
August 17	Nothing has changed.
August 18	At the other end of the street.
August 19	Write about the silent treatment.
August 20	Write about stealing time.
August 21	Write about an overheard remark.
August 22	You picked up a hitchhiker.
August 23	Write about something that made you cry.
August 24	Write about being on the inside.
August 25	Write about the morning after.
August 26	Write about what has yet to happen.
August 27	You are in the backyard.
August 28	Write about a dangerous ride.
August 29	My mother once told me…
August 30	"…and her red hair lit the wall." (after Richard Hugo)
August 31	"It's my belief we're all crazy." (after Trudy, the bag lady)

$\mathcal{S}$eptember

September 1 Write a December memory.

September 2 "It was Sunday morning."
(after Sharon Olds)

September 3 Write about your neighborhood at 5 P.M.

September 4 You eavesdrop on a conversation.
What do you hear?

September 5 The time between dusk and dawn.

September 6 Write about a fragrance.

September 7 Write about a place you long for.

September 8 _____ is the color I remember.

September 9 Write about a car trip.

September 10 Write about a time someone went too far.

September 11 I don't remember.

September 12 In a cemetery.

September 13 There's a bar in Austin, Texas, called
Jake's Place.

September 14 Write about someone who sinned.

September 15	"For as long as she lives, and probably longer, she will never forget his face." (after Alison Moore)
September 16	Write about something you would do differently.
September 17	Write about a purchase.
September 18	It's raining now.
September 19	Write about a time someone lost control.
September 20	Accept loss forever. (after Jack Kerouac)
September 21	Write a daydream.
September 22	"In the blue night frost haze..." (after Gary Snyder)
September 23	Write about a time someone surprised you.
September 24	Write about a door key.
September 25	Write about a simple pleasure.
September 26	Night is falling. You're not at home.
September 27	Write about a time the lights went out.
September 28	Write about a time you did something out of superstition.
September 29	The night won't save anyone.
September 30	Write about a rendezvous.

October

October	1	On the night train to _____.
October	2	Write about never and always.
October	3	Write about taking a detour.
October	4	Three things my father told me.
October	5	Write about a fragment.
October	6	Write about small mistakes.
October	7	You're in a café.
October	8	Losing control.
October	9	"_____ are my weakness." (after Pam Houston)
October	10	"In those days..." (after Roger Aplon)
October	11	It was as far as I could go.
October	12	Write a summer memory.
October	13	Write about a pillow.
October	14	Write about being in a closed space.

October 15	Write about promises made.
October 16	You're driving in your car.
October 17	When I opened my mouth to sing.
October 18	Write about a hideout.
October 19	Write about jealousy.
October 20	Someone says, "Can I see you in the kitchen?"
October 21	Write about a bruise.
October 22	I come from . . .
October 23	These are the lies I told you.
October 24	There is a place called _____.
October 25	Write about small scrapes and bruises.
October 26	Write about "what goes without saying."
October 27	Write what the darkness proposes.
October 28	"It was a summer of blue-black nights." (after Don DeLillo)
October 29	"I'm at a loss . . ."
October 30	"What will happen can't be stopped." (after Ann Beattie)
October 31	Write about someone who has passed to the other side.

November

November 1   Write about casting a spell.

November 2   I dreamed _____.

November 3   Write about yearning.

November 4   The sun is rising.

November 5   Write about divine intervention.

November 6   You're eating breakfast.

November 7   Secretly, I know my name is _____.

November 8   Write about electricity in the air.

November 9   It's what I do at 2:30 in the morning when I can't sleep.

November 10   Write about where rivers join.

November 11   Write about a song you love.

November 12   This is what can happen when _____.

November 13   "The window had other views."
              (after Wislawa Szymborska)

November 14	Remember an afternoon.
November 15	Write about what's obvious.
November 16	Write about the last night of _____.
November 17	Write of something done in a small moment.
November 18	These were the reasons to stay.
November 19	Write about being lost along the way.
November 20	Write about the booth in the corner.
November 21	Returning takes too long.
November 22	Write about a hesitation.
November 23	Write about being underwater.
November 24	Write about opening a gift.
November 25	Write about the fault line.
November 26	This is what was left when he was gone.
November 27	Write about a sudden storm.
November 28	One Saturday night...
November 29	Write about avenues of escape.
November 30	A woman named _____.

December

December   1   Write about an invitation refused.

December   2   ...and nobody objected.

December   3   I recall that evening together.

December   4   Write about an unforeseen friendship.

December   5   Write about a series of mishaps.

December   6   This is what she said.

December   7   Write about hard times.

December   8   Write about winter constellations.

December   9   Behind lace curtains.

December 10   Write about seeing someone for the last time.

December 11   Write about a late night phone call.

December 12   I carried it in my pocket.

December 13   This is the difference between men and women.

December 14   Write about a street you lived on.

December 15   Write about a red convertible.

December 16	"I walked into the Maverick Bar in Farmington, New Mexico." (after Gary Snyder)
December 17	Write about a redheaded woman.
December 18	Write about masks.
December 19	You are in a church.
December 20	Write what you didn't say.
December 21	Write about a scar.
December 22	It's Sunday morning. The phone rings.
December 23	Write about something you want but cannot have.
December 24	Write about a fire.
December 25	"We ate Chinese."
December 26	Write about something sacred.
December 27	Write about a time someone told you a secret.
December 28	If I tell you the truth...
December 29	These are the delicacies of a ruined evening.
December 30	A random light.
December 31	In anticipation of the night.

If a writer is constantly concerned with truth,
grace, order, and other verities,
his inner life just naturally enriches
in proportion to his working.

— William Saroyan

You can't sit
around thinking.
You have to sit
around writing.

— David Long

The way to find
your true self is
by recklessness
and freedom.

— Brenda Ueland

If you don't risk
anything, you
risk even more.

— Erica Jong

Writing is always a
voyage of discovery.

— Nadine Gordimer

Writing is a kind of
free fall that you
then go back and
edit and shape.

— Allan Gurganus

You must be
unintimidated by
your own thoughts
because if you
write with some-
one looking over
your shoulder,
you'll never write.

— Nikki Giovanni

The role of the
writer is not to say
what all can say
but what we are
unable to say.

— Anaïs Nin

Facts can
obscure the truth.

— Maya Angelou

Anyone can
become a writer.
The trick is
staying a writer.

— Harlan Ellison

I write out of
curiosity and
bewilderment...

— William Trevor

I don't feel like a
novelist or a
creative writer as
much as I feel like
an archaeologist
who is digging
things up and
brushing them off
and looking at the
carvings on them.

— Stephen King

The world is made up
of stories, not atoms.

— Muriel Rukeyser

Everything we learn
to write is a stepping
stone for the next
level of conversation
we are capable of
having with
ourselves.

— Christina Baldwin

The trick is to make
time—not to steal it—
and produce fiction.

— Bernard Malamud

I honestly think in
order to be a writer,
you have to learn to
be reverent.

— Anne Lamott

If I knew what was
going to happen
next, I wouldn't be
able to write. I
wouldn't be
interested in writing.

— Walker Percy

As I write I create
myself again and
again.

— Joy Harjo

If you write a
hundred short
stories and
they're all bad,
that doesn't mean
you've failed. You
only fail if you
stop writing.

— Ray Bradbury

Truth is such a
rare thing, it is
delightful to tell it.

— Emily Dickinson

All I am is the
trick of words
writing themselves.

— Anne Sexton

It's all about letting
the story take over.

— Robert Stone

I find that I actually
have to write in
order to discover my
ideas. I think you
could allow yourself
to never get started
if you tried to guess
in advance what was
going to inspire you.

— Jay McInerney

Talent isn't enough.
You need motivation—
and persistence too:
what Steinbeck called
a blend of faith and
arrogance.

— Leon Uris

An incurable itch
for scribbling takes
possession of
many and grows
inveterate in their
insane hearts.

— Juvenal

I'm a writer.
I don't cook and
I don't clean...

— Dorothy West

I will go so far as to
say that the writer
who is not scared is
happily unaware of
the remote and
tantalizing majesty
of the medium.

— John Steinbeck

The writer gleans
wind scraps; he
listens wherever he
can. Each day is full
of instances; what
counts, as with all
stimuli, is the
sympathetic response.

— Nicholas Delbanco

If we had to say
what writing is,
we would define
it essentially as
an act of courage.

— Cynthia Ozick

You develop a style
from writing a lot.

— Kurt Vonnegut

Rationality squeezes out
much that is rich and
juicy and fascinating.

— Anne Lamott

Language alone
protects us from the
scariness of things
with no name.

— Toni Morrison

Much of my writing is
energized by unresolved
memories—something
like ghosts in the
psychological sense.

— Joyce Carol Oates

There's a suspense
in the process of
writing which I've
learned to be both
charmed and
faintly, decently—
terrified by.

— John Barth

I write. The longer I
live, the more con-
vinced I've become that
I cultivate my truest
self in this one way.

— Tom Chiarella

The novels have
been written in
order to find some-
thing out about
what I was think-
ing, questions I was
asking myself that I
needed to answer.

— May Sarton

Finding the
stories is not the
hard part. Writing
them down is.

— Annie Proulx

Writing is love,
a mission, and a calling,
and how and where and
why you write are
very crucial issues.

— Lynn Sharon Schwartz

You write about what
you know or you
write about what
you want to know.

— Jill Ciment

To be a good
writer, you not
only have to write
a great deal, but
you have to care.

— Anne Lamott

*nit*cance and value.

I shall live badly
if I do not write.

— Françoise Sagan

lar ried: others must decide

Teach yourself to
work in uncertainty.

— Bernard Malamud

Start to write,
and let one thing
lead to another.

— Ring Lardner

To honor our
dreams and to
honor our loved
ones and to honor
our rituals and our
lives is precisely
what literature is
endlessly trying
to teach us.

— Allan Gurganus

It is my heart that
makes songs, not I.

— Sara Teasdale

If one writes about
oneself, the real motive
must be, I think,
to give reassurances to
other people.

— Christopher Isherwood

The impulse for much
writing is homesickness.
You are trying to get
back home, and in
your writing you are
invoking that home, so
you are assuaging the
homesickness.

— Joan Didion

What one has written

If you're going to be
a writer, you first of
all have to develop
unusual powers of
observation.

— Nadine Gordimer

at one has written is not to be

You have to give
yourself the space
to write a lot with-
out a destination.

— Natalie Goldberg

I write to understand as
much as to be understood.
Literature is an act of
conscience. It is up to us
to rebuild with memories,
with ruins, and with
moments of grace.

— Elie Wiesel

Only those that risk
going too far can
possibly find out
how far one can go.

— T. S. Eliot

You can't depend
on your eyes when
your imagination
is out of focus.

— Mark Twain

You do your best work
when you're not
conscious of yourself.

— Peter Matthiessen

The hardest trade in
the world is the
writing of straight,
honest prose about
human beings.

— Ernest Hemingway

Every person you
meet—and every-
thing you do in life—
is an opportunity to
learn something.
That's important to
all of us, but most of
all to a writer
because a writer can
use anything.

— Tom Clancy

Easy reading is
damned hard writing.

— Nathanael West

I'm a real believer
in research, but I
have a funny way of
doing it. I think
you should write
first and then do
the research.

— Mona Simpson

I started to discover
I was being more
honest when I was
inventing, more
truthful when
dreaming.

— Michael Ondaatje

You know what
images are important
because they hit you
so powerfully. But
you don't always
know what they mean.

— Gloria Naylor

You have to know
what you're doing
when you turn your
life's stories into
fiction. You have to
be immensely daring,
very skilled and
imaginative, and
willing to tell every-
thing on yourself.

— Raymond Carver

With good writing,
I think, the most
profound response
is finally a sigh,
or a gasp,
or holy silence.

— Tim O'Brien

The main thing is
to write a lot, to
keep yourself
immersed in the
element of poetry,
to stay deep in
the creative
possibilities.

— James Dickey

You're a writer and that's something better than being a millionaire—because it's something holy.

— Harlan Ellison

I think the writer
must serve the
inarticulate.

— Nelson Algren

Don't be afraid of giving
yourself away for if you
write you must. And if
you can't face that,
better not write.

— Katherine Anne Porter

Some people don't really
bother much with
remembering; it seems
such a useless activity.
But most writers are
addicted to it.

— Alice Munro

Those rituals of
getting ready to
write produce a
kind of trance.

— John Barth

A poem begins as a lump in the throat, a sense of wrong, a homesickness, a lovesickness...It finds the thought and the thought finds the words.

— Robert Frost

The unconscious
creates, the ego
edits.

— Stanley Kunitz

Follow your inner
moonlight; don't
hide the madness.

— Allen Ginsberg

The necessity of the idea creates its own style. The material itself dictates how it should be written. A writer must express himself in the most honest, truthful manner he can.

— William Faulkner

I never know when I
sit down, just what
I am going to write. I
make no plan; it just
comes, and I don't
know where it
comes from.

— D. H. Lawrence

Follow your image
as far as you can.
Push yourself.

— Nikki Giovanni

Think of yourself as
an incandescent
power, illuminated,
perhaps, and forever
talked to by God
and his messengers.

— Brenda Ueland

One of the few things I
know about writing is
this: spend it all, shoot
it, play it, lose it, all,
right away every time.

— Annie Dillard

Don't think of
literary form. Let
it get out as it
wants to. Overtell
it in the matter of
detail—cutting
comes later. The
form will develop
in the telling.
Don't make the
telling follow
the form.

— John Steinbeck

It's a great relief
to me to know
that I can actually
be creative and be
happy at the
same time.

— James W. Hall

You're the first audience
to your work, and the
most important audience.

— Gloria Naylor

In a very real sense, the writer writes in order to teach himself, to understand himself, to satisfy himself. The publishing of his ideas, though it brings gratification, is a curious anticlimax.

— Alfred Kazin

You're told time
and again when
you're young to
write about what
you know, and
what do you know
better than your
own secrets?

— Raymond Carver

I put a piece of paper
under my pillow, and
when I could not sleep I
wrote in the dark.

— Henry David Thoreau

Eighty percent
of success is
showing up.

— Woody Allen

All good writing is
built one good line
at a time. You
build a novel the
same way you do a
pyramid. One
word, one stone at
a time, underneath
a full moon when
the fingers bleed.

— Kate Braverman

The writer's first affinity is not to a loyalty,
a tradition, a morality, a religion, but to life itself,
and to its representation in language.

— Jayne Anne Phillips

Recommended Reading

This list includes just a few of the many books about writing in general — the attitude and philosophy of writing, rather than instructions on the craft. But there are dozens of really good books about the craft, too. Also included in this very abbreviated list: some of my favorite books with writing exercises. After you've finished these, I urge you to visit your library or your bookstore and browse the stacks.

Bradbury, Ray. *Zen and the Art of Writing*. New York: Bantam Books, 1992.

Cameron, Julia. *The Artist's Way: A Spiritual Path to Higher Creativity*. Los Angeles: J. P. Tarcher, 1992.

Dillard, Annie. *The Writing Life*. New York: Harper and Row, 1989.

Epel, Naomi. *The Observation Deck: A Tool Kit for Writers*. San Francisco: Chronicle Books, 1998.

Goldberg, Natalie. *Wild Mind: Living the Writer's Life*. New York: Bantam Books, 1990.

_____. *Writing Down the Bones: Freeing the Writer Within*. Boston and London: Shambala, 1986.

Heffron, Jack. *The Writer's Idea Book*. Cincinnati: Writer's Digest Books, 2000.

King, Stephen. *On Writing: A Memoir of the Craft*. New York: Scribner, 2000.

Lamott, Anne. *Bird by Bird: Some Instructions on Writing and Life*. New York: Pantheon Books, 1994.

Lerner, Betsy. *The Forest for the Trees: An Editor's Advice to Writers*. New York: Riverhead Books, 2000.

Rekulak, Jason. *The Writer's Block: 786 Ideas to Jump-Start Your Imagination*. Philadelphia: Running Press, 2001.

Sher, Gail. *One Continuous Mistake: Four Noble Truths for Writers*. New York: Penguin/Arkana, 1999.

Ueland, Brenda. *If You Want to Write*. St. Paul, Minn.: Gray Wolf Press, 1987.

Wooldridge, Susan G. *Poemcrazy: Freeing Your Life with Words*. New York: Clarkson Potter, 1996.

About the Author

Judy Reeves writes fiction, nonfiction, and drama, and teaches creative writing workshops across all genres. She is the co-founder of The Writing Center, a nonprofit literary arts organization. Among other books, she is editor of the *Brown Bag Anthology*, a collection of writings originating in her twice weekly writing practice groups. As a member of the Second Story Writers, a women's writing ensemble, two of her plays have been produced. Judy lives in Barcelona, Spain, where she is at work on a novel.

Books by Judy Reeves

A Writer's Book of Days:
A Spirited Companion and Lively Muse for the Writing Life

Writing Alone, Writing Together:
A Guide for Writers and Writing Groups

New World Library
is dedicated to publishing books and other media
that inspire and challenge us to improve
the quality of our lives and our world.

For a catalog of our fine books and audios, contact:

New World Library
14 Pamaron Way
Novato, CA 94949

Telephone: (415) 884-2100
Fax: (415) 884-2199
Toll-free: (800) 972-6657
Catalog requests: Ext. 50
Ordering: Ext. 52

E-mail: escort@nwlib.com
www.newworldlibrary.com